Penny for your Thoughts:
NY v Daniel Penny

by Matthew Russell Lee

Inner City Press

November, 2024

TABLE OF CONTENTS

Chapter 1: A Subway Car Like This One

Chapter 2: Suppression Hearing, October 3, 2024

Chapter 3: Homeless History

Chapter 4: 100 Centre Street

Chapter 5: The Bronx

Chapter 6: Severe Mental Illness/ Change the World with Tupac

Chapter 7: The Warrant

Chapter 8: Opening Arguments, Nov. 1, 2024

Chapter 9: Rosario and the White Man, November 4, 2024

Chapter 10: The People's Timeline

Chapter 11: Sanchez and the Nike Witness, November 7, 2024

Chapter 12: Lenox Hill Hospital Record

Chapter 13: The Trainer Caballer, November 14, 2024

Chapter 14: Marine Corps Martial Arts Program

Chapter 15: The Brain Dies First, November 15, 2024

Chapter 16: Medical Examiner Harris, November 18, 2024

Chapter 17: The Autopsy - Chapter 18: Texas and TikTok

Chapter 19: Character Witnesses: J6 and Guns, Nov. 19, 2024

Chapter 20: Penny's Medical Examiner Chandru, Homicide on Cross, Studies, Tasers & Texas / Sunny Side Up

I. A Subway Car Like This One

Onto a subway car like this one he got on, a muffin in his jacket pocket wrapped in plastic, a spleen speckled, it would turn out, by sickle cell disease. But that is not what killed him, Assistant District Attorney Dafna Yoran would say.

Was it an improper blood choke, or the terror he inspired, in a lady from Park Slope with her baby, a Nike brand ambassador on the way to Rucker Park? Even the Bronx school girls said they were frightened, even if one did later drop the dime on the white man. That was prosecutor Jillian Shartrand's doing, to call the victim by his name and the defendant merely the white man.

Of the decedent there was more, not only the mother stuffed in a suitcase but the channeling of Michael Jackson, dreams.

Now to see a man lifeless on the subway's floor, liquids flowing out of his pants, his eyes rolling back -- here in the courtroom, a woman starts to cry and the anonymous jurors look over, a lady in a COVID mask, her eyes suddenly big.

Another woman next to me is typing loudly, two fingers only, stopping to fan herself and shake her head. It is not possible to know if she is for a guilty or not guilty verdict: either way, she doesn't like it.

The defendant sits stiffly straight, not looking at the jurors. A Marine who misapplied the air choke? A racist or a hero or both. The subway door is closing. The story nears its end.

II. Suppression Hearing, October 3, 2024

[Penny is sitting at defense table, his video interview is being played. These interchanges are from the interview]

Police: The doors close and he's still yelling - when does he throw the jacket?

Penny: He said, I'll kill you, this and that.

Penny: Afterward, the cop came. I asked the people on the train to stick around, the cops are going to come. I'm not out here trying to attack. That's not me, that's not how I was trained. This guy was saying he's going to kill people, he's prepared to go to jail

Police: Did he go up to particular people?
Penny: He's saying, I'm going to kill you.
Police: He doesn't put his hands on anyone?
Penny: He's threatening people. I'm trying to keep him from hurting people.

Police: This whole interaction happens from one train stop to the next?
Penny: Yes.
[Two police get up and leave. Penny remains sitting, in baseball hat.]
[Here is courtroom: We are forwarding to 4:58]
[Police re-enter]
Police: You put him in the hold?
Penny: Yes

Penny: He's grabbing on.
Police: You hold him in that position from one stop to the next. You said two males came up?
Penny: Yes and I let him go. [Gestured with his hands]
Police: He's still moving?
Penny: Yes.

Police: He's still yelling?
Penny: Yes.

Penny: He's yelling he's going to kill someone, he wants to go to jail forever.
Police: Did he have his hands in his pocket?
Penny: No - his hands were out. [Gestures]
Police: You need anything? Cigarette?

Penny: How long is this whole process?
Police: We want to talk to you.
Penny: So I am detained?
Police: Yes.
Penny: I would like an attorney.
[Here is courtroom: We are stopping the video]

[Now questioning of Police Officer on the stand, here in courtroom]
Counsel: Did you ask Officer Tejada if he spoke to any witnesses?
Police Officer: No.
Counsel: There was no dispute between Mr. Penny and Mr. Neely, as far as you know?
Officer: There was not

Counsel: What is the process for you to gather the information from the officers on the scene, so you can assess the case?
Detective: One by one.
Counsel: Did you do that here?
Detective: I did not.

Penny's lawyer: Detective, part of your job is to notate your investigation in a DD-5, is that correct?
Detective: Yes
Penny's lawyer: Isn't it true that Sergeant Johnson contacted you about what occurred between Mr. Penny and Mr. Neely?
Detective: I don't remember

Penny's lawyer: In your DD-5, you called it an "Unusual Occurrence," right?
Detective Medina: That's what the form says, when something like this happens.
Penny's lawyer: Something like what?
Detective Medina: It's a possible homicide.

Penny's lawyer: Every homicide is unusual?
Detective Medina: Yes.
Penny's lawyer: At some point reviewed a

video of the struggle between Mr. Penny and Mr. Neely?
ADA: Objection!
Judge: Overruled.
Detective Medina: Yes. After.

Detective Medina: The DA's Office said they wanted to get involved and attend
Penny's lawyer: Do you know if Mr. Penny was informed of Mr. Neely's death while he was at the precinct?
Det Medina: No sir.
Penny's lawyer: Was he informed during the interview?
A: No.

No further questions.
Judge: The court is going to take ten minutes to stretch its legs.

[They've back, with responding Police Officer on stand]
ADA: What did you see when you entered the train car?

Police Officer: There was a male on the floor.
ADA: What was his condition?
Police Officer: He looked homeless, from his clothes. He was unconscious.

ADA: What were you told?
Police Officer: That the individual had come onto the train threatening people.
ADA: Who told you that?
Police Officer: A white male. Over there, in the grey suit.
Judge: Indicating the defendant.

ADA: Is this your body camera footage?
Police Officer: Yes.
[Video plays: Penny and another man stand over Jordan Neely, on the ground]
ADA: Who is the other officer?
Police Officer: Sergeant Johnson.

[On video, officers turn over the body of Jordan Neely]
ADA: Did you interview any witnesses?
Police Officer Tejada: No.
ADA: No further questions.
Penny's 2d lawyer: The subway car was

mostly empty?
Officer Tejada: Yes.

Penny's 2d lawyer: Did you learn that the people on the platform had been on the car and witnessed what occurred between Mr. Penny and Mr. Neely?
ADA: Objection!
Judge: Overruled.
Officer Tejada: Yes.

Judge: Wait, our TV screen shorted out, there's some smoke
[#NYCourts]
Judge: There's going to be an acrid smell but we have the air conditioning on, let's keep going.
Penny's 2d lawyer: Mr. Penny said he didn't know of Mr. Neely had a weapon?
Officer Tejada: Yes

Penny's 2d lawyer: What did you find in Mr. Neely's jacket pocket?
Officer Tejada: A muffin. A full muffin.
Penny's 2d lawyer: You saw the muffin top... Was Mr. Neely still breathing?

Officer Tejada: Seemed like it. He had a pulse too.

Penny's 2d lawyer: You didn't do CPR for several minutes, right?
Officer Tejada: We didn't.
Penny's 2d lawyer: But you did use NARCAN, right?
ADA: Objection! Relevance!
Judge: I'll allow it for now.
Officer Tejada: Yes

Next witness is Officer Kang of the 5th Precinct.
ADA: Where did you work before?
Officer Kang: In a hotel.
ADA: What did you get a call for?
Officer Kang: Assault in progress, Broadway Lafayette station. We went down to the uptown F train platform

ADA: Did you speak to the defendant?
Officer Kang: Yes. I asked, How exactly did he end up in this state? He gestured with his arms, like a choke.
ADA: What did you do?

Officer Kang: We turned him over, sunny-side up, we gave him chest rubs. I did feel a pulse

ADA: Let me play you your body-worn camera footage
[Video: running past a Marc Jacobs poster and down onto the platform - then police putting on rubber gloves, standing over Jordan Neely. Penny approaches and says, He threw shit, hands them his wallet and ID

Penny's 2d lawyer: Was CPR initiated right away?
Officer Kang: No.
Penny's 2d lawyer: Why not immediately?
Officer Kang: I felt a pulse.
Penny's 2d lawyer: You spoke with an African American woman, a witness?
Officer Kang: I don't remember her description

Penny's 2d lawyer: What did she say?
ADA: Objection! Irrelevant!
Judge: Overruled.
Officer Kang: How he was acting, leading up

to the choke hold.

Penny's 2d lawyer: What did she say about how Mr. Neely was acting?

Officer Kang: Erratic. Maybe other details

Officer Kang: At some point my supervisor Sergeant Johnson told Mr. Penny, you have to come back to the 5th Precinct with us.

Penny's 2d lawyer: Was Danny told he had to stay on the train?

Officer Kang: Yes.

Penny's 2d lawyer: No Miranda warnings?

Officer Kang: No

Penny's 2d lawyer: You're not a detective, right?

Officer Kang: I am not.

Penny's 2d lawyer: So you had to relay information up the chain. The witnesses you spoke to, did you take pedigree information?

Officer Kang: Yes.

Penny's 2d lawyer: Two witnesses were taken to the precinct, right? A white woman and an African American woman?

Officer Kang: Yes.

Penny's 2d lawyer: Let me show you the video

[Two women shown. One says, He was saying, Kill.. and It wasn't a choke hold

Penny's 2d lawyer: It sounded to you like the witnesses were taking the side of Mr. Penny, talking about how threatening Mr. Neely had been?

Officer Kang: Yes.

Judge: We'll break here.

The testimony that Jordan Neely initially had a pulse when NYPD arrived, and there was no immediate CPR - but rather NARCAN - drew reactions in the courtroom, as did the questioning of Penny before any Miranda warning.

III. Homeless History

It was suggested to Kurt Wheelock that he should write a profile - a "spiritual profile," they called it - of someone on the soup line whom he'd met. Would it be J.C., the wild man who after three days sober drinking tea in the kitchen could be found in the middle of Houston Street, high on Mad Day 20/20, later having even his shoes stolen as he lay on the sidewalk near Ludlow Street?

Maybe J.B., the soft-spoken man also an alcoholic, who defecated on himself and mumbled thanks as the priests of Holy Name hosed him down?

Kurt focused on Gary Lieb, a less effusive man he helped up to Bellevue Hospital one night, and waited with him from midnight to five am. Then Kurt had to leave, to head downtown to make soup.

Apparently Gary Lieb wandered out of Bellevue Hospital soon after Kurt Wheelock left. He was found frozen to death on a construction side on First Avenue. His family, rich as it turned out, cursed Kurt for negligence. But where were they?

Kurt asked himself, where had he been?

The answer, at least literally, was in the soup kitchen. And what was that accomplishing? Kurt had started to wonder. He moved on.

IV. 100 Centre Street

In 100 Centre Street there are any number of criminal cases, crimes of violence. Jordan Neely, it emerged, testified at the trial for his mother Christie's death, against her boyfriend and killer who was representing himself, having studied to be a paralegal. Jordan was cross-examined by the killer. And now his death would be the subject of cross-examination.

…"At trial, defendant decided to represent himself and the trial judge directed his assigned public defender to serve as standby counsel. At the conclusion of the testimony, defendant moved for an acquittal, or in the alternative, a new trial and the judge denied both motions. The judge sentenced to thirty years in prison on the murder charge."

They run a tight ship in 100 Centre Street
As the building collapses around them
The Sergeant is big but lets the Press in
While the lady in white yells Be quiet!

In fact, Jordan Neely had been in 100 Centre Street on February 9, 2023, two stories below on the 11th floor, before Judge Ellen Biben. For felony assault - punching a 67-year old woman and breaking bones in her face - he got an "alternative to incarceration" - transport to Harbor House in The Bronx.

V. The Bronx

Kurt, too, had been in The Bronx - his second Post Office box was at HUB station on St Ann's Avenue and Westchester Avenue, just north of 149th Street. It was surrounded by vacant lots, and across the street from an abandoned brewery. Kurt and Fritz went in there, too, with the magazine. There were guys living in the old brewery, fixing or stripping stolen cars, piling up metal in shopping carts to roll to Hunts Point and sell for scrap.

Kurt met a guy name Robert who had an entire empty building, the whole block on 152nd Street and Melrose Avenue, in which he stored all the metal he collected, sometimes the pipes from buildings that were not yet abandoned, but soon would be. Kurt told him he didn't have to live alone, he could be hooked up with wood stove heat, and electricity from the street lamp, up in their flagship homestead on Crotona Park East.

But I want to live alone, Robert replied. Kurt could relate, and yet couldn't relate.

VI. "Severe and Persistent Mental Illness"/ Changing the World with Tupac

The defense managed to get into evidence, and circulate to the press as the prosecutors do, an exhibit consisting of a Bellevue visit by Jordan Neely in December 2021:

"28 year old male, undomiciled, with Schizophrenia and a history of polysubstance abuse (notable K2)… Prior civilian psychiatric admissions, presenting with recent K2, cannabis and alcohol use. The current working diagnosis is acute exacerbation of severe and persistent mental illness.

"He was repeatedly insisting he is not supposed to be in the hospital and is not safe here [REDACTED] because he had changed the world with Tupac Shakur, and that now his life is in danger.

August 2015: Mr. Neely was interviewed this morning. He volunteered that Tupac Shakur has used him to change the world

January 2017: Patient became agitated and paranoid toward the end commenting "that's some Michael Jackson shit, they saw one of my videos and they were jealous. Patient also reported there to be 'sexual stuff' going on in CPEP as to why he became agitated there.

January 2021: "Patient stated 'I'm cold and don't have anywhere to go right now because the subways are closed.'"

VII. The Warrant

Jordan Neely left Harbor House in The Bronx on February 22, 2023 - and the next day, Judge Biben issued a warrant for his arrest.

As its last exhibit, the defense would put this warrant into evidence.

VIII. Opening Arguments, November 1, 2024

Daniel Penny and his two lawyers have just walked into this 13th floor courtroom.
Judge: Off the record, does the Defense intend to make an opening today?
Penny's counsel: Yes.
[Through the windows, chants from down on Centre Street] Drum roll...

Judge: The defense moved to introduce parts of some statements witnesses made to officers that were captured on body-worn camera, just after the incidence. The Court has reviewed some - they may be excited utterances, others not

Judge: There was a witness named Ms. Rosario at 2:38 pm, I can see most of it coming in except the last part where she was asked by the officer, Did it look like he was on drugs - I don't think that will come in

Judge: Likewise a Mr. Latimer, he displays emotion and excitement with only light questioning by the officer... Ms. Giddons on Sergeant Brito's camera, that seems excited

ADA: The whole Q&A?

Judge: I think so - there was no question about being on drugs

Judge: Anything else before the jurors enter? I noticed the demonstrations this morning, they are audible in the robing room and elsewhere - I will admonish the jurors not to pay attention. Bring in the jury

Jury entering!

Judge: Happy to see you, jury selection is over. This is the People of the State of New York against Daniel Penny, he is charged with manslaughter in the second degree and criminally negligent homicide, Jordan Neely.

Judge: Anyone who wants to take notes, raise your hand. [Most jurors do] It is a short week next week [no trial on Election Day, or Wednesday either] We'll begin with the People.

ADA: Good morning jurors. Jordan Neely took his last breaths on a dirty floor

ADA: Jordan Neely was homeless and mentally ill. On May 1, 2023 he demanded to be seen. He walked in - he talked about being hungry. He made threats about hurting people and wanting to go to jail for life. Daniel Penny took it upon himself to neutralize him

ADA: The defendant kept Mr. Neely in a deadly chokehold. When Mr. Neely naturally tried to break free, Mr. Penny applied more pressure. When he let go, Mr. Neely was in the last stages of the dying process. The defendant had killed him - permanently silencing him

ADA: Deadly physical force such as a chokehold is only permitted if necessary. The defendant went waaaay too far. His indifference toward Mr. Neely caused him to needlessly kill him. In contravention of law and human decency, the defendant did not try to defuse

ADA: He was indifferent to Mr. Neely's humanity. He is charged with manslaughter in the second degree, and criminally negligent homicide if he failed to perceive the risk. You will hear from many people on that northbound F train. At 2d Ave, Jordan Neely got in

ADA: He was ranting, but at no one in particular. He said he would kill anyone, that he was ready to go back to jail for life. The witnesses were like you - young girls, not young girls, men with criminal records. They will say Mr. Neely did not show a weapon

ADA: Despite the fact that he did not display a weapon or direct his threats at any particular person, people began to move away. Still some people felt trapped. The defendant, a former Marine - he told detectives he wasn't scared for himself, he protected others

ADA: The defendant went for the jugular without trying other ways of defusing. The defendant's arm was wrapped about his neck, his legs around his torso. Mr. Neely was thrashing. At 2:23:30 the train arrived at Broadway-Lafayette, we'll show from i-Track.

ADA: The defendant told the exiting passengers to call the police. There was no one left on the train for the defendant to protect. Mr. Penny knew that Mr. Neely was not armed. Mr. Neely did not pull out any weapons while trying to pull out of defendant's chokehold

ADA: The defendant did not ask people to check if he was armed. So he clearly knew Mr. Neely was not armed. But with no one in real danger, the chokehold continued, five minutes and 53 seconds. For some he was resisting. Yvette Rosario filmed from the platform

ADA: Yvette Rosario, a 17 year old girl, filmed with her cell phone - it shows Mr. Penny's hand on Mr. Neely's. One minute and 52 second after the train arrived, a Mexican journalism named Juan Alberto Vasquez entered the car. His 5 minute video is critical

ADA: You will see how unnecessary this chokehold was. Two able bodied men were there. Mr. Neely was 6 foot one inch, but skinny. The count was three on one. You will not meet the person on the right, a German tourist who refused to return to NY

ADA: The defendant did not let go until 2:29. When he is released, he is limply lying on the floor. You will learn Defendant had specialized training in chokeholds
[mic and speaker begin to echo]
Judge: Our electronics are not great. Please continue.

ADA: The defendant's own trainer will testify there are two kinds of chokeholds: blood choke, and the air choke. The first stops the blood from going into the head - pass out in 8 to 13 seconds. In training, they are only allowed five second. The person can tap out

ADA: A Green Belt Marine like the defendant knows that. But he continued for 51 seconds. The air choke, it's the front of the neck. The trainer will tell you this is not recommended, there is a danger you will damage their air ways. Oxygen can't reach their brain

ADA: The defendant's was a combination of blood choke and air choke. The defendant was aware he was unconscious. Mr. Gonzalez will tell you he felt Mr. Neely go limp. You'll see when he let go, he left Mr. Neely on the floor and didn't look back. He got his hat

ADA: He was aware of the risk and did it anyway. That falls below the standard of care required of a reasonable person. But why? Why was the defendant so reckless with another person's life? The judge will tell you that's not something we have to prove

ADA: We will show you that Mr. Penny did not recognize Mr. Neely's humanity. He did not try to revive him. The defendant is a Marine trained in First Aid. He just stood, waiting for the police to arrive. He was unconcerned about Mr. Neely's welfare

ADA: He told the officers that Mr. Neely had been threatening everyone and "I just put him out." Unapologetically. He said it while Mr. Neely was on the floor. Obviously it was likely he was going to die. Why did he not see Mr. Neely's humanity? Appearance or more?

ADA: As for Jordan Neely, nothing could be done to save him. The police officers did not give up on him. Then the EMTs showed up, trying for 26 minutes. He was pronounced dead at the hospital. You will hear from the Medical Examiner he died from the chokehold

ADA: You will hear evidence about mental illness, and sickle cell, largely benign. This trial is not a referendum on the timeliness of the police's response or our society's failure to deal with mental illness on the subway. It is about, was he criminally reckless

ADA: We'll ask you to find the defendant guilty.

Judge: Jurors, I'll give you some time.

They've back.

Daniel Penny's lawyer Thomas Kenniff: This is about a man doing what we would all like done for us. Threats to kill people, in the closed confines of a moving subway car, you either bury your head and pray, as some did, or you stand up and protect

Penny's lawyer: Danny grew up on Long Island, then enlisted in the Marines. They he enrolled at City Tech in Brooklyn to study architecture. He taught swimming, and rode the subway every day. He had finished his morning classes - the train was crowded

Penny's lawyer: Danny is headed to the gym on 23rd Street, he doesn't get off at 2d Ave as usual. He puts on his ear buds. A seething, psychotic Jordan Neely come on and announces his presence. Danny thinks, he's just high on drugs. But this was different

Penny's lawyer: Mr. Neely throws his jacket on the floor, makes demands and takes on a fighting stand. He says, give it or I'll take it. Concern turns to fear. He's talking about going back to Rikers, being ready to die. Neely is moving up the subway car, lunging

Penny's lawyer: Neely sets his sights on a bench of female passengers. Danny sees a mother with a child behind a stroller, Neely says, "I will kill." There was no opportunity to de-escalate, spill a soda or anything. Danny leaps into action, left arm over shoulder

Penny's lawyer: You will hear witnesses call Danny and his conduct respective, non-aggressive, meant to protect. But Jordan Neely did not want the police to come - he had an active warrant out for his arrest. He aggressive resists

Penny's lawyer: As you watch the video I need you to put aside your emotions. That video will not capture the whole story, the first two minutes, the fear he instilled. Danny can barely contain Jordan Neely because he is resisting so aggressively.

Penny's lawyer: Neely appears to give up - then explodes again. Even with two other man, Danny must struggle to contain him. Then a 1st call gets through to the police dispatcher. There is no call to them calling Danny as the aggressor. But the police are nowhere

Penny's lawyer: Jordan Neely did not say, "I can't breathe." Danny pleaded with onlookers to call the police. He was concerned Mr. Neely would summon another burst. Mr. Gonzalez, the dark-skinned man you see on the video, confirms this: a 5 minute struggle

Penny's lawyer: The burden of proof is on the government. The evidence will point to cardiac arrest due to drugs, or sickle cell. Danny did not apply pressure on his neck for a length of time to cause death.
[Sips water]

Penny's lawyer: Danny sought to protect those not able to protect themselves. He is not a killer, he is not guilty of any homicide. We'll ask you to find him not guilty. Thank you.
Judge: First witness?
ADA: The people call witness Tejada

Judge: Mr. Tejada, welcome.
ADA: Officer, how long have you been with NYPD?
Tejada: Five years. I was a public safety officer with the 5th precinct.

[Jury being shown shaking body-worn camera video of Officer Tejada running into Broadway-Lafayette subway station, past a Marc Jacobs ad, onto the platform. Penny: He came on, [scared the] shit out."
ADA: You said call a bus?
Tejada: Ambulance.
[People's Exhibit 1.]

AUSA: What is Sgt Johnson doing?
Tejada: Administering Narcan
[All of the police officers now have on bright blue gloves, yellow and black Tasers visible in their holsters.
Jurors staring intently at the video screen.
Judge is standing with his arms crossed]

ADA: I'm going to stop showing the video at this point. Let me show you some more exhibits. [Prosecutor hands photos first to the defense, then to witness Tejada; looks out over courtroom gallery.]
ADA: It was Car 9774?
Tejada: Yes.
ADA: No further questions.

Judge: Cross?
Penny's lawyer: The call you got for the radio run mentioned a gun?
Tejada: Yes.
Penny's lawyer: Then about someone harassing people on the subway - a male Black, correct?
Tejada: Yes.

Penny's lawyer: You suspected the perp had a gun?

Tejada: Yes.

Penny's lawyer: You recovered an item from Mr. Neely's jacket pocket?

Officer Tejada: Yes, a muffin.

[Small laugh from somewhere in the courtroom]

Penny's lawyer: You got to the subway 6 to 7 minutes after you got the call for the radio run?

Tejada: Yes

Penny's lawyer: No one tried rescue breaths on Mr. Neely, correct?

Tejada: No one did.

Penny's lawyer: But they tried Narcan before CPR, right?

Tejada: I don't remember the sequence.

Penny's lawyer: It took ten more minutes for EMS to come?

Tejada: I believe so.

Penny's lawyer: Danny remained on the scene and cooperated with officers, correct?

Tejada: Yes.

Penny's lawyer: Didn't appear he had anything to hide?

Tejada: No.

Penny's lawyer: Did you speak with bystanders?

Tejada: No.

Judge: We'll break.

Some questioned the impact of jurors hearing the chants from Collect Pond Park. Jurors 2 and 7 wore COVID masks. Penny's lawyer was more schmoozy with the witness, and with the jury. Will it work?

IX. Rosario and the White Man, Nov 4, 2024

Daniel Penny just walked into courtroom, in gray suit.
Clerk: All jurors are here.
Judge: Great.
[Several of the NYC Courts officers overseeing this courtroom are the same ones from the Trump criminal trial

Penny's lawyer: The Defense wanted to bring up an exception, that should prompt the Court to revisit its prior seal ruling on Mr. Neely's prior bad acts... The People said Mr. Neely just wanted to be "seen" - to engender sympathy. It weaponized the court's ruling

Penny's lawyer: Mr. Neely was not looking to be heard- he was looking to hurt people, as sealed evidence shows. So allowing the People to make an opening statement that he was just someone trying to be seen is very problematic. There are good reasons to ignore him

Penny's lawyer: The prior acts speak to what Mr. Neely thought when he entered that subway car. Was he bent on hurting people, as he had done and tried to do several times that week. The People went too far, and we are being prohibited from presenting our defense

Judge: I'll stick to my ruling. I disagree. I don't think the People weaponized my ruling. But I'll look at it and if I change my mind I'll let you know. Bring in the jury.
Jury entering!
ADA: The People call Yvette Mercedes Rosario... How old are you?
Rosario: 19

ADA: How long have you lived in NYC?
Rosario: Ten years.
ADA: And before that?
Rosario: Dominican Republic.
ADA: On the train that day, were you in the

end?

Rosario: In the middle.

ADA: How full was it?

Rosario: It wasn't packed

ADA: What happened before the doors closed?

Rosario: He came in, what's his name, Jordan, he took off his sweater and said he was homeless, he didn't have any money, he didn't care about going back to jail.

ADA: How did he come in?

Rosario: He stopped the door

ADA: Where did he throw his sweater?

Rosario: It didn't land on any one.

ADA: Did he touch anyone?

Rosario: I didn't see that, no. No weapons.

ADA: What did you do?

Rosario: I was very nervous. I got scared by the tone of what he was saying, an angry tone.

Rosario: I have seen things on the train but not like that. I wanted the door to open. But the train was moving. I heard a sound.

ADA: What did you see?
Rosario: The white guy was holding on to Mr. Neely. Like this-
ADA: The witness has placed her arm on her neck

ADA: When you saw the white man holding on to Mr. Neely, how were they?
Rosario: His arm on his neck.
ADA: Where is Mr. Neely's back with respect to the white man? Was Mr. Neely lying on top of the white man?
Rosario: Like this. He had him held. The doors opened

Rosario: I did have a video.
ADA: Where were you standing?
Rosario: Outside the car.
ADA: Did the white man's arm ever leave Mr. Neely's neck?
Rosario: Not that I saw. The police told us to go. Me and my friend we took the D train. Jordan was not moving

Rosario: They had told me-
Penny's lawyer: Objection [hearsay]

Judge: Sustained.

ADA: Let me show you Exhibit 2E
[Shaky video from platform shown, with shouting]

ADA: Did you hear someone yell, He's dying, you gotta let him go?
Rosario: Can you play it again?
[It is played again]
Rosario: I hear it no on the video but I did not hear it then.
ADA: Do you know you yelled that?
Rosario: I don't. I just wanted to leave

ADA: What the white man still holding on to Jordan's neck?
Rosario: Yes.
ADA: People's Exhibit 7a - where are the white man's legs?
Rosario: I don't know.
ADA: 7b, another still, what's this?
Rosario: He's holding him
ADA: Exhibit 8 - when was this?
Rosario: After

ADA: I don't believe I have any more questions.
Judge: Cross?
Penny's lawyer: Yes... Good morning, may I call you Yvette? I am Thomas. You recognize Mr. Penny?
Rosario (looks) Yes.
Penny's lawyer: You call Mr. Neely Jordan - but did you know him?
Rosario: No.

Penny's lawyer: In the same way, you learned their names after?
Rosario: The Marine, that's what I knew.
Penny's lawyer: The prosecutor kept calling him "The White Man." I'm going to call him Danny, is that OK?
Rosario: OK.

Penny's lawyer: You came and met the DAs?
Rosario: Yes.
Penny's lawyer: You testified to the grand jury?
Rosario: Yes.
Penny's lawyer: I'm going to ask you about

that. But on the train, Mr. Neely threw his jacket?

Rosario: It was a sweater.

Penny's lawyer: He said he was not afraid to go back to Rikers Island jail?

Rosario: Yes.

Penny's lawyer: You recall him saying, Someone is going to die today?

Rosario: Yes. I buried my head on my friend's shoulder.

Penny's lawyer: Then you couldn't see

Rosario: I could not see.

Penny's lawyer: When you did see Mr. Neely, did he look angry?

Rosario: Yes.

Penny's lawyer: Did you pray for the doors to open?

Rosario: Yes.

Penny's lawyer: Could you tell if Danny was squeezing Mr. Neely's neck?

Rosario: No...

Penny's lawyer: You were scared Mr. Neely might get up again?

Rosario: I was

Penny's lawyer: You told the 911 operation it was Mr. Neely causing trouble?

Rosario: Yes.

Penny's lawyer: Did you hear Danny says, Calm down?

2d ADA: Objection?

Judge: 1 lawyer per exam

Penny's lawyer: Let me show you detective's notes from your previous answers. Do you recall, Calm down, calm down?

Rosario: I don't remember that.

Penny's lawyer: Is it possible you said that?

Rosario: I don't know.

Penny's lawyer: No further questions.
Break

X. The People's Timeline

2:23:00 PM F train departs Second Avenue subway station People's Exhibit 6 "I-TRAC" MTA Transit Report 0:30

2:23:30 PM F train arrives at Broadway-Lafayette subway station People's Exhibit 6 "I-TRAC" MTA Transit Report 0:30

2:24 PM Ivette Rosario video begins recording People's Exhibit 7 and 7c Still frame from 17 second timestamp in video shows a phone displaying the time 2:24 PM 1:22

2:25:22 PM Juan Alberto Vasquez full-length video begins recording People's Exhibit 10 and 12 Vasquez Phone Extraction and Vasquez Handheld Video 0:58

2:26:20 PM First 911 call People's Exhibit 19 Headings Report (911 Message 001) 2:12

2:28:32 PM Jordan Neely's last voluntary movement People's Exhibit 10, 12, and Dr.

Cynthia Harris Testimony Vasquez Phone Extraction and Vasquez Handheld Video 0:51

2:29:23 PM Daniel Penny lets go of Jordan Neely People's Exhibit 10 and 12 Vasquez Phone Extraction and Vasquez Handheld Video 0:56

2:30:19 PM Juan Alberto Vasquez full-length video ends People's Exhibit 10 and 12 Vasquez Phone Extraction and Vasquez Handheld Video 3:36

2:33:55 PM PO Tejada enters the subway car and observes Jordan Neely on the floor of the subway car People's Exhibit 1 BWC of PO Tejada 3:55

2:37:50 PM Officers begin administering CPR on Jordan Neely People's Exhibit 1 BWC of PO Tejada 1:17

2:39:07 PM Daniel Penny exits subway car with PO Ortiz People's Exhibit 30 BWC of PO Ortiz 7:51

2:46:58 PM EMTs from Northwell arrive on scene and take over administration of CPR to

Jordan Neely People's Exhibit 14 BWC of PO Ziemkiewicz 52:02

3:39:00 PM Jordan Neely is pronounced dead at Lenox Hill Greenwich Village Hospital People's Exhibit 43 Jordan Neely Medical Records

XI. Sanchez and the Nike Witness, Nov 7, 2024

Jury entering! [Two have on COVID masks]
Clerk: People versus Daniel Penny!
Judge: Welcome back. Next witness.
ADA: We call Moriela Sanchez....Where do you live?
Sanchez: Harlem.

ADA: How often do you ride the subway?
Sanchez: Often
ADA: On the day in question, what train were you on?
Sanchez: The F train. My friend and I were standing.
ADA: Were seats open?
Sanchez: No.
ADA: What happened?
Sanchez: (taps fingers) The train was moving

Sanchez: Jordan threw his jacket down. He took near Penny.
ADA: Did it hit anyone?
Sanchez: No.

Judge: You called him Jordan, did you know him before?
Sanchez: No.
Judge: And you called the defendant Penny - did you know him?
Sanchez: No.

ADA: What did Jordan say?
Sanchez: That if no one gave him food he was going to attack.
ADA: But did he say it to anyone in particular?
Sanchez: No.
ADA: What happened next?
Sanchez: After that Penny put his hands around his neck

Sanchez: Penny dropped down with his hand around his neck, Jordan was on top of him.
ADA: While they were on the ground, where did Penny have his arms around Jordan? [Sanchez gestures]
ADA: For the record, she touched the sides of her neck

ADA: What happened when the train got to Broadway Lafayette?
Sanchez: He was still holding him. Then a man in a black hat was holding his legs down.
ADA: What was Jordan's condition?
[Person in gallery behind me starts crying loudly]

[Person - African American woman - goes out into the hall. In courtroom, crying still audible]
Judge: Ms. Sanchez, please speak louder.
ADA: Did you see Jordan move again?
Sanchez: No. I took a video.
ADA: Let me show you a still from it
[Blurry subway photo shown

ADA: Are you able to actually see them in this picture?
Sanchez: No.
[More members of the public are let into the courtroom - there is a line out in the hall]

ADA: I'll play your 9-1-1 call.
[Sanchez' voice: He's trying to attack everyone -

911 Operator: What does he look like?
Sanchez: He's black. They're holding him down

ADA: I'll show this video
[Video is through subway car window, from the platform. Police officers in bright blue gloves lean over Jordan Neely]
ADA: I have no further question for this witness.
Judge: Any cross?
Penny's lawyer: Thank you. Good morning Ms. Sanchez

Penny's lawyer: May I call you Mariela?
Sanchez nods.
Penny's lawyer: Would it be fair to say Mr. Neely was screaming?
Sanchez: Yes he has.
Penny's lawyer: You were frightened, right, that he would make good on his threat?
Sanchez: I was.

Penny's lawyer: He got very close to other people, did he not?
Sanchez stares at courtroom ceiling.

Penny's lawyer: As close as 1 foot?
Sanchez: I don't know.
Penny's lawyer: You met with the DA's office - and last May you testified to the grand jury?
Sanchez: Yes

Penny's lawyer: You told the grand jury, He was like one feet away. He was like right there.
Sanchez nods.
Judge: You have to say yes or no.
Sanchez: Yes.
Penny's lawyer: No one's trying to put you on the spot.
[Sanchez is crying, her head in her hands]

Judge: Ms. Sanchez, are you OK?
Sanchez nods, crying
Penny's lawyer: Nice and slow. You tell me if it's too fast... Who were you trying to protect Yvette [friend, previous witness] from - Jordan?
Sanchez: Yes.
Penny's lawyer: He said he wanted money?
Sanchez: Yes.

Penny's lawyer: It looked like Danny was trying to stop Jordan from hurting people?
Sanchez nods, staring down.
Penny's lawyer: And that's what you said in your 911 call?
Sanchez nods.

Penny's lawyer: You didn't think Danny was holding him too tight? You did?
Sanchez seems to nod.
Penny's lawyer: But you previously said, He was holding him to stop him from hurting people, not to hurt him.
Sanchez: I said that.
Penny's lawyer: We're almost done

Penny's lawyer: Your previously said, He was trying to protect people so he wouldn't hurt nobody.
Sanchez: I said that.
Penny's lawyer: Then you met with these prosecutors, about what you would say here?
Sanchez: Yes.
Penny's lawyer: I have no further questions

Next witness is a Nike employee who says she lives in Brooklyn, names seems to be Caedryn Schrunk.
ADA: Before NY, where are you from?
Nike witness: The Midwest. I came here for my career. I'm a brand manager
ADA: Where were you sitting?
Nike witness: In the middle

ADA: What did you see?
Nike witness: A man coming toward us, yelling. I noticed his smell as well. I assumed he was having a mental issue. I witnessed the scent
ADA: You mentioned he was gesturing. How?
Nike witness: His hands were complimenting what he was saying

Nike witness: It was very traumatic, it was very believable, that this would happen.
ADA: What did he say?
Nike witness: Life threatening claims for his own life too, I don't care if you die, kill me,

lock me up - it was so believable, it was like a Satanic belief

Nike witness: It was hot. I truly believed I would die. You were fearful. Everyone was frozen. I thought it was the moment I was going to die.
ADA: Where was he?
Nike witness: Very close to me.
ADA: Did he approach anyone in particular?
Nike witness: I did not see

ADA: What happened next?
Nike witness: Someone came behind him and took him down.
ADA: Do you see him?
Nike witness: Over there in a blue suit and red tie.
Judge: Witness had identified the defendant.
ADA: How did he move?
Nike witness: Quickly.

ADA: After you got out of the train car, what did you see?
Nike witness: Two other men were over him, one holding his legs.

ADA: Can you describe Mr. Neely's condition at this point?

Nike witness: His legs were still like wobbling a bit. That's all I can recall.

ADA: Show me where he was, and you were, the touch screen should work
[Witness draws an M on bench, an X on floor]
No further questions.
Cross.
Penny's lawyer: About this diagram. Can I call you K/Caitlin?
Witness: Yes

Penny's lawyer: This is where you saw the woman protecting her baby in the stroller?
Witness: Yes. He was moving
Penny's lawyer: Would it be fair to say, Adrienne, that the last thing you saw before Danny took him down was he moving toward the lady and baby?
Yes

Penny's lawyer: You take the train a lot?
Nike witness: Yes, out to the communities for

events.

Penny's lawyer: You get the unlimited monthly Metrocard?

Nike witness: I do.

Penny's lawyer: And you see a lot?

Nike witness: I've seen men throwing themselves around

Nike witness: But this was the worst. I felt like I was going to die.

[Commotion in back.

Court Security: Quiet down!]

Nike witness: It took over the subway, soiled sweatpants. A very strong odor.

Penny's lawyer: Did you see the back of his pants?

A: Soiled

Penny's lawyer: After Danny took him down, did you feel safer?

Nike witness: Yes. The danger was less.

Penny's lawyer: Did you feel it would have been safe for Danny to let him go at that point?

ADA: Objection!

Judge: Overruled.
Witness: Absolutely not

Penny's lawyer: Did you think he was on drugs too?
Nike witness: Yes. I had never seen anything like it.
Penny's lawyer: You saw him on the ground for some period of time - did he appear calmed down?
Nike witness: He was squirming and trying to actively get up

Penny's lawyer: Did you ever hear him gasp or say I can't breathe?
Nike witness: No.
Penny's lawyer: Did you think Mr. Neely could die?
Nike witness: I had no thought that that would happen.
Penny's lawyer: When Danny releases him, was there still movement?
Yes.

Penny's lawyer: How long did it take the police to arrive?

Nike witness: Ten to fifteen minutes. It seemed like quite a while.
Penny's lawyer: Did they question you?
Nike witness: Yes. At the 5th precinct.
Penny's lawyer: Was it video recorded?
Yes.
No further Qs

Re-direct
ADA: You didn't see Mr. Neely from behind at first - but you say his pants were soiled in back?
Nike witness: Yes. I saw it later.
ADA: But you couldn't see the back
Penny's lawyer: Objection! This is her witness, your Honor.
Judge: Overruled.

Witness: I saw his pants later. Smelled.
Break

XII. Lenox Hill Hospital Record

Narrative History Text: 02F2 WAS DISPATCHED TO A CARDIAC ARREST. UPON ARRIVAL THE CREW FOUND AN APPROXIMATELY 30 Y/O MALE LAYING ON THE GROUND SUPINE PULSELESS AND APENIC.CPR WAS INITIATED BY PD. AED WAS APPLIED. APPROPRIATE OPA WAS APPLIED. PT AIRWAY WAS PATENT. BREATHING WAS BEING VENTILATED VIA BVM AT 15 LPM. CIRCULATION INTACT, NO BLEEDING, CTC WAS WARM DRY AND PALE. 01W2 ASSUMED PT CARE. HEENT INTACT. CHEST INTACT. ABDOMEN SOFT AND NON TENDER X4 QUADRANTS. PELVIS IS STABLE. PT WAS TRANSFERRED INTO THE AMBULANCE VIA BACK BOARD THEN TRANSFERRED TO THE STRETCHER. PT WAS TRANSFERRED TO THE

NEAREST HOSPITAL WITHOUT INCIDENT.

Unable to Sign: Unable to Sign Reason: Deceased

XIII. The Trainer Caballer, Nov. 14, 2024

[Juror 11 was more than an hour late. Now:]
All rise!
Judge: Welcome back. We are going to begin by replaying some video.
[On screen, subway car at an angle]
ADA: This is People's Exhibit 28
[Witness: I guess he was pissed, he said he don't care about going to jail

Judge: Next witness.
ADA: The People call Joseph Caballer.
Witness entering! [Dude has a mohawk, suit jacket and white shirt, no tie]
ADA: Where do you work?
Caballer: A cement plant. Prior I was a water restoration technician, and a kickboxing instructor, Marine

ADA: Where were you deployed?
Caballer: Cuba, Bahrain, Spain, Japan...
ADA: What training did you receive in martial arts in the Marines?

Caballer: The techniques, tan belt to green belt.
ADA: Do you know Daniel Penny.
Caballer: He was with me in Expeditions

ADA: Did you instruct him in martial arts?
Caballer: Yes, for a time, on ship...
ADA: What did you last communicate with him?
A: He texted me to talk to his lawyers.
ADA: What level did Mr. Penny attain?
A: Green belt.
ADA: Is this the manual you used?
A: Yes.

ADA: What'd be the result of a proper choke?
Caballer: Rendering unconscious, then release pressure.
ADA: What is a blood choke?
A: Pressure to artery, cut blood flow to brain.
ADA: When you were choked, what did it feel like?
A: Breathing through a crushed straw

ADA: What is an air choke?
Caballer: Trachea, cut air flow to lungs.

ADA: There are precautions, Appendix A.
[Six photos of chokeholds shown to jurors]
ADA: Now let's apply it to this case. What does this show?
A: In this hold, the figure 4 was not done correctly

Caballer: He's pressing on the windpipe.
ADA: Could it cause damage?
A: Yes.
ADA: Here's Exhibit 7a, a still from the Rosario video. What is Mr. Neely doing?
A: Trying to grab Mr. Penny's arm.
ADA: What's this?
A: An attempt at the figure 4 variation.

ADA: Now let's go frame by frame
[Super slow motion video shown
Caballer: That elbow is not centered.
ADA: Now this still from his interview [in small room in 5th Precinct]
Caballer: Now he is demonstrating the correct figure 4 variation, left hand on right bicep

ADA: No further questions.
Judge: Cross?

Penny's 2d lawyer Steven Raiser: You trained your fellow Marines that in a real world situation if a person goes unconscious you release the pressure, not the hold?
Caballer: It depends. The situation dictates.

Penny's lawyer Raiser: In this photo, it may be there is no pressure being applied to the trachea?
Caballer (pauses) Correct.
Raiser: In training you do sparring and grappling?
A: Yes.
Raiser: Sometimes the grip can shift, correct?
A: It can.

Penny's lawyer Raiser: To do a blood choke you have to have access to both sides of the neck?
Caballer: Yes.
Raiser: You trained that if pressure is removed, and even if grip remains, the people can come back to consciousness?
A: Correct.

Penny's lawyer Raiser: Here, does the man in the black hat have a role?
Caballer: Mr. Penny is in control. Where the head goes, the body follows. The guy in the black hat is still grabbing his arm.
Raiser: Does it appear safe to let him go?
A: I don't know

Penny's lawyer Raiser: Does it look like he's applying pressure here?
Caballer: No. He is looking up and talking to the two people...
Raiser: No further questions.
Judge: Re-direct?
ADA: He still had Mr. Penny's head, right?
Caballer: Yeah.

ADA: Nothing more.
Judge: We'll break.

Things grew worse for the prosecution on cross-examination, and even more so on redirect, when the ADA was forced to ask, But isn't it possible? Never a good question, when beyond a reasonable doubt is needed. But there's time, the judge made clear - in fact the trial may go long: on Nov 14, Juror 11 (seemingly a woman with white hair) was a full hour late. In the press gallery, a reporter (not this one!) gesticulated and fanned herself. It's getting hot...

XIV. Marine Corps Martial Arts Program

Rear Ground Choke

The rear ground choke is a blood choke that is performed when you are behind the aggressor on the ground. Technique ~ Begin by sitting on the ground with the aggressor sitting between your legs with his back to your chest. ~ Place your lower legs over the aggressor's thighs, this should be done simultaneously or after the choke is executed in order to prevent a counter. Do not cross your ankles at any time, this will compromise your position and places you in a vulnerable position to counterattack. Use your insteps and toes to create constant pressure on the aggressor's thighs.

Note: Do not try to get your toes under the aggressor's legs. ~ With your left arm, reach up and grab the aggressor's forehead and pull back. ~ With your right arm, reach over the aggressor's right shoulder and hook the bend between the forearm and bicep of your arm around his neck. Ensure that the aggressor's windpipe is positioned within the bend of your arm and that pressure is not being exerted directly on his windpipe. ~ With your left hand, palm side up, clasp both hands together, palm-to-palm. Exert pressure with your biceps and forearm on the carotid arteries on both sides of the aggressor's neck; while maintaining pressure, draw the aggressor closer to you by drawing your right arm in.

- To increase the effectiveness of the choke, apply forward pressure to the back of the aggressor's head with your head by bending your neck forward. Stretch out the aggress Figure-4 Variation of Rear Choke The figure-4 variation of the rear choke is also a blood choke and is performed when you are behind the aggressor.

Technique - Follow steps one through three for the rear choke. - Grasp your left bicep or shoulder with your right hand and place your left hand against the back of the aggressor's head. - With your left hand, push the aggressor's head forward and down. - Draw your right arm in, maintaining pressure with your biceps and forearm on both sides of the aggressor's neck. - To increase the effectiveness of the choke, stretch the aggressor out by straightening and arching your body while maintaining your leg and arm positions.

XV. The Brain Dies First, November 15, 2024

Jury entering!
Judge: Jurors, the defense is going to offer an exhibit about the NYPD questioning a witness, Mr. Clay. The defense will enter a portion of the police report.
Penny's lawyer Steve Raiser: May I explain to the jury?
Judge: Yes.
[redacted NYPD report]

Penny's lawyer Raiser: Mr. Clay said, I wondered, what does this guy have on him? What does he have in his pocket?
Judge: OK.
Witness entering!
ADA: Before we get into your opinion of the cause of death, compression of the neck, what did you get?
A: Lab report

ADA: What did you find in the decedent's blood?

Dr. Harris: Synthetic cannabinoids... K2.
ADA: Was the amount of synthetic cannabinoids in Mr. Neely's body quantified?
Dr. Harris: No. Nor the timing of ingestion. We were informed he was a chronic user

Dr. Harris: We also found that Mr. Neely had sickle cell disease.
ADA: Did you review videos?
Dr. Harris: Yes.
ADA: Did anything you reviewed alter your conclusion on the cause of death?
Dr. Harris: No. It either corroborated my original conclusion or irrelevant

ADA: We'll show you the video
Judge: The monitor facing the audience is not turned on.. We'll proceed, but put in a call.
ADA: What is happening here?
Dr. Harris: I'm told here Mr. Neely was speaking
Penny's lawyer: Objection!
Judge: Overruled

ADA: Please explain air hunger.
Dr. Harris: Inability to expel carbon dioxide.

It is unpleasant to genuinely terrifying.

ADA: On this slide, what do you see?

Dr. Harris: Mr. Neely's face is turning purple. Compared to his arms.

ADA: Back to the video, at 1:35

Dr. Harris: The brain is 2% of the body's weight, but uses 20% of the oxygen. When it is in distress, it sends out signals... I believe at this point he had lost consciousness but was still twitching... Watch his feet.
His pants are wet. I think he has urinated

Dr. Harris: At Mr. Neely's autopsy I found 330 ML of urine. He had a full bladder.

ADA: What about defecation?

Dr. Harris: It's a similar principle.

ADA: You were told this individual felt a pulse?

Dr. Harris: I was.

ADA: How was that possible?

A: Makes sense

Dr. Harris: The brain dies first. A pulse is maintained for up to 10 minutes, in cases like a hanging or a drowning or a chokehold. The heart has its own automaticity - that's why we can do organ donation.

ADA: So the pulse - does it change your finding?

A: No

Dr. Harris: He had a normal heart in a dying body.

ADA: Let's turn to the autopsy.

[Photograph of eyes, opened by pincers, shown to jury]

Dr. Harris: Those are pools of blood...And these are the vocal cords

[Some jurors strain toward the screen; others recoil]

Judge: We'll break.

Expert Harris was setting out to prove a case, as to cause of death, standing and using a pointer, walking around the photos shown on the large monitor. But at least one close daily observer, predisposed toward guilt, opined that the

state hasn't proved its case - "yet," they added. But will they?

XVI. Medical Examiner Harris, November 18, 2024

Before jury comes in
Penny's lawyer Kenniff: We think the NYPD DD5 should not come in.
Judge: I think the People are correct that some of this should come in, Mr. Latimer's statements. But all of Para 2 must come in. It shows where "screaming male" comes from

ADA: We don't think Paragraphs 3-5 need to come in.
Judge: I think they do.
ADA: We want to keep out his statement about the amount of force he should would be necessary. That's up to the jury.
Judge: I'll cure that in my limiting instruction

Jury entering!
Penny's lawyer Steve Raiser: Did you speak with the ADAs about this cross?
ME Harris: On some points.
Raiser: Which?
Dr Harris: To make it clear about Mr. Neely's

breathing. Raiser: Did you speak about sickling?

Dr. Harris: Not over the weekend

Penny's lawyer Raiser: Pull up GX 31, the PowerPoint- can you really say these scratched on the neck are from Mr. Neely's own finger nails?

Dr. Harris: In the video, he's grasping for his neck. So to me it was the most likely. But there could be other explanations

Penny's lawyer Raiser: For example, the scratches could have come from intubation, right?

Dr. Harris: Yes. Although the injuries I see from that tend to have a more blunt force trauma look to them, where the tube makes contact.

Penny's lawyer Raiser: Didn't you hear one of the police officers say Mr. Neely was still breathing?

Dr. Harris: I don't think so

Raiser: It he wakes up breathing, it's significant, right?

Dr. Harris: It might appear so to a lay person. It's neurological posturing

Penny's lawyer Raiser: Police Officer Tejada said he was breathing, and so did another officer in the background, right?
Dr. Harris: I watched the video without audio. I wasn't interested in that.

Penny's lawyer Raiser: Didn't an EMT say, He was conscious?
Dr. Harris: I'm most interested in my own observations.
Raiser: You're saying the chokehold triggered a sickle cell crisis?
Dr. Harris: Many professional athletes have sickle cell and this does not happen

Penny's lawyer Raiser: Let's talk about the K2
Dr. Harris: K2 can cause cardiac arhythmia
Raiser: And acute respiratory crisis?
Dr. Harris: There's research on that. Some use NARCAN
Raiser: You received a genetic report on Mr. Neely's heart?
Dr. Harris: I did

Penny's lawyer Raiser: You get paid more the more advance in your career, right?
Dr. Harris: On longevity.
Raiser: How much do you make now?
Dr. Harris: I'm not sure... Like $175,000. I've worked the last three weekend in a row for this.
Raiser: We all have that

Penny's lawyer Raiser: You testified that it didn't matter in Mr. Neely had enough K2 in his system to kill an elephant, your finding would be the same?
Dr. Harris (pauses) Yes.
Raiser: The grand jury has the right to ask for evidence?
Dr Harris: I guess

Penny's lawyer Raiser: You testified to the grand jury on June 6, 2023, right?
Dr. Harris: Yes, but could I have my binder?
Raiser: I'm going to put it up on the screen... Didn't you make an error on your resume of when you got promoted?
Dr. Harris: Yes.

Dr. Harris: It had to do with then doctor change over, everyone jokes about not getting operated on on July 3, that's when the new doctors start.

Penny's lawyer: Nothing was going to change Chief Grant's mind?

ADA: Objection!

Judge: What did he say?

A: Not to wait

Judge: We'll break.

Penny's lawyer dug into whether Dr. Harris had made up her mind, why she didn't listen to the audio from the police bodycams, and if she tailored her testimony to getting promoted and more pay. She didn't seem to like the questions - who would? - but it was cross. Some of her answers could be taken to mean she came to see it one way, and became attached to it

XVII. The Autopsy

M-23-013065 JORDAN MAURICE CAINE NEELY

OFFICE OF CHIEF MEDICAL EXAMINER CITY OF NEW YORK REPORT OF AUTOPSY CASE NO. M-23-013065

"I hereby certify that I, Cynthia Harris, M.D., City Medical Examiner-I, have performed an autopsy on the body of Jordan Maurice Caine Neely, on the 2nd day of May, 2023, starting at 9:00 AM in the Manhattan Mortuary of the Office of Chief Medical Examiner of the City of New York. This autopsy was performed in the presence of Dr. Stuelpnagel.

EXTERNAL EXAMINATION: The body is received in the supine position in a plastic body bag, which is secured with a white plastic seal bearing the number 345066. A handwritten OCME tag encircles the right wrist. A digital hospital band encircles the right wrist. A digital hospital tag encircles the left first toe.

The body is that of a well-developed, well-nourished, average-framed, 6'1", 165 lb. (BMI: 21.8 kg/m2), medium-brown-skinned man, whose appearance is consistent with the reported age of 30 years. The scalp has curly, black hair, which measures up to 1/2". There is a 1/2" mustache and 1/2" beard. There are no palpable facial fractures. The eyes have brown irises and slightly congested conjunctivae. The left earlobe is pierced once but is free of jewelry. The atraumatic oral cavity has natural teeth in good condition. The anterior and posterior aspects of the torso are normally developed. The atraumatic external genitalia are those of a circumcised adult man. The testes are descended and free of palpable masses. The anus is atraumatic with soft brown stool soiling the perianal region and the buttocks.

The extremities are free of edema or linear scars overlying subcutaneous veins. There is a 1/2" hyperpigmented patch of skin on the volar right forearm. The atraumatic fingernails are ill-kempt with black-brown soiling beneath the nails. There are hyperpigmented calloused burns of the fingertips of the right first and second fingers. The distal right second finger has an adhesive bandage; the cuticle beneath is torn. There are many crusted abrasions of the chest, upper back, shoulders, proximal arms, buttocks, and legs. These abrasions range in size from 1/16" to 1-1/2", range from punctate to irregularly oval to linear in shape, and appear in various stages of healing

XVIII. Texas and TikTok

Dunchie flew in from Texas
To help his friend Danny on trial
The ADA studied her cell phone
Was the gun in the TikTok really his?

It's different in Texas, said Kenniff
Asked of a Dunchie conviction
Out in the hall Dunchie cut out
Culture war even in court

XIX. Penny's Character Witnesses: J6 and Guns, Nov 19, 2024

Come to order!
Judge: Off the record, could the lawyers come up real quick?
[Whispered sidebar]
Judge: At the bench, we talked about whether the public can view exhibits. I delegate that to the parties. The DA's office has not been prompt in making them available

Judge: The defense wants to put on witnesses to speak about what awards he got as a Marine. The DA's Office opposes this strenuously. In this case honesty is at issue, as is reputation for empathy, also at issue regarding his regard for the deceased

Penny's lawyer Thomas Kenniff: I have 21 years of military service myself. These awards are not given for specific acts of valor. The humanitarian award speaks to the Marine's conduct, it's heavily based on reputation. I cite People v. Valdez, 1st Dept 2008

Penny's lawyer Kenniff: Their Marine trainer witness implied that my client is willing to disregard his training. So our witnesses are relevant. They've made his Marine service part of the rubric of this case. They are free to cross-examine

ADA: There are principles of law more important than Mr. Kenniff's feelings. This is outrageous. He should have asked earlier. He cites only on case - a case in which the People elicited from their witness testimony about military valor. The judge called it wrong

ADA: We say that he did not see Mr. Neely's humanity - in that moment. It is not a question of character evidence. Yet they get to call six character witnesses? It's excessive. But to spring this on us, military records, there's no basis

Judge: I've heard enough. The People have a point - this should have been raised during jury selection -

Penny's lawyer Kenniff: We got these records -

Judge: 'm going to take a break and make up my mind.

Come to order!

Judge: This should have been brought up prior to trial. Nevertheless, character evidence is only allowed about reputation for certain specific traits. Military commendations don't speak to that, other than the humanitarian award. So, no exhibits

Judge: But the defense can question about certain characteristics, that's it. Nothing on good conduct awards or medals, anything like that.

Penny's lawyer Kenniff: I need a few minutes to talk to the witnesses so they avoid your trip wires.

Judge: Go ahead

[Kenniff exits, comes back]
ADA: We want to reargue. This award is not about reputation. I really don't want any more from Mr. Kenniff about his feelings, if he can't describe the award accurately.
Judge: I'm allowing it.
ADA: Wait - it was an award to a platoon

Penny's lawyer Kenniff: Your Honor-
Judge: You've got your ruling, Mr. Kenniff. Bring in the jury.
Jury entering!
Kenniff: Defense calls Nolan Drylie. State of residence?
Drylie: I live in Alabama
Kenniff: Welcome to New York. 1st time?
Drylie: Seen the Rockettes

Penny's lawyer Kenniff: What do you do down there?
Drylie: Farming. Timber. Chicken and eggs.
Kenniff: You're familiar with Mr. Penny?
Drylie: I was his Sergeant in the Marines. It's like a family. Honor, courage and commitment. Empathy, compassion

Penny's lawyer Kenniff: What kind of Marine was Danny?
Drylie: Above reproach.
Kenniff: Did he have a reputation for following Marine Corps training?
Drylie: Yes he did.

Judge: Cross.
ADA: On your Facebook 12 days after Mr. Penny was charged, you called on Marine brothers to ride to New York, right?
Drylie: Support and father.
ADA: You wrote, this is for a true homie - if you have a negative opinion, unfollow me. Let me show you

ADA: You were going to ride your motorcycle as an angry protest against our state, right?
Penny's lawyer Kenniff: Objection! Protest against our state?
Judge: Overruled, I'll allow it.
ADA: April 6, 2023, you wrote, Men, be toxically masculine again

ADA: You said Mr. Penny got the medal for empathy - that's not true is it?
Drylie: It was for his actions after a hurricane in North Carolina.

Next witness is Gunnery Sergeant Dunchie
Penny's lawyer Kenniff: Where are you from?
Dunchie: Texas. I was born in Baltimore.
Kenniff: First time in NY?
Dunchie: First time staying this long.
Kenniff: How do you know Danny?
Dunchie: I was his platoon sergeant.

Penny's lawyer Kenniff: To succeed in the Marines did Danny have to treat people equally?
ADA: Objection!
Judge: I'll allow it.
Dunchie: Absolutely.

Judge: Cross?
ADA 2: You flew here from Texas on Mr. Penny's dime?
Dunchie: From Vermont.
ADA 2: Your user name on TikTok is "the Dunch LOL" - and you feature a weapon you

own there?
Dunchie: Yes.
ADA 2: A gun in a fanny pack - you point it at the camera?

Penny's lawyer Kenniff: Objection!
Judge: I'll allow it.
Dunchie: Yes.
Judge: Cross
Kenniff: The attitude to guns is different in Texas than NY?
Dunchie: Definitely.
Kenniff: Are you a criminal?
Dunchie: No.
Kenniff: Are you motivated by 2 night in Marriott?
A: No

Next witness is Steve Strachan, of Suffolk County, New York. He's an airline pilot.
Penny's lawyer Kenniff: What are your hobbies?
Strachan: Golf, surfing - I saw Danny on the beach, we caught some waves, he was very inviting. It's hard to make new friends at 33.

Penny's lawyer Kenniff: Did Danny help integrate you into the surfing community at Gilgo Beach?
Strachan: Yes. East coast surfing, there's long periods without waves, he would help me fix up my home-
ADA: Objection!
Judge: I'll allow it.
Strachan: We went sailing

Penny's lawyer Kenniff: Do you see Danny a lot?
Strachan: We'll he's been busy lately [some laughter here in the courtroom]
Kenniff: Does he have the reputation of being a peaceful and calm person?
Strachan: Yes.
Judge: Any questions by the People?
ADA: No cross

Judge: We'll break here

Gunnery Sergeant Dunchie is African American; he looked directly at jurors as he answered Kenniff's questions. In the TikTok video raised by ADA 2, he shows only the butt of the pistol - then raises his eye brows, in a Nike cap. The next character witness, a (white) pilot and Gilgo Beach surfer, the ADAs had no questions for.

XXI. Penny's Medical Expert Chandru, Direct, Nov 21, 2024

Penny's lawyer Steven Raiser: Doctor, let me show you Defense Exhibit J
Penny's medical expert: This is a diagram of the circulation of blood in the body.
Raiser: This will help explain circulation given the sickle cell trait?
Doctor: Yes it will...

Penny's lawyer Raiser: Doctor, did you rule out the choke hold as the cause of death of Jordan Neely?
Penny's medical expert: I did
Raiser: If a person is not rendered unconscious by the chokehold, it can't be the cause of death, right?
Penny's medical expert: Yes

Penny's lawyer Raiser: How does sickle cell crisis death work?
Penny's medical expert: The cells are starved of oxygen
Raiser: How is it different from a chokehold

death?

Penny's medical expert: Sickle cell crisis is an internal phenomenon in the body.

Penny's lawyer Raiser: Let's do some hypos - a person is high on K2, and psychotic, and is restrained and dies. Also, a person is in a sickling crisis and is restrained and dies. Are these chokehold deaths?

Penny's medical examiner: No.

Penny's medical expert: Doctor Harris was just speculating.

Penny's lawyer Raiser: Is that an appropriate way to determine a cause of death?

Penny's medical expert: No.

[Vasquez video shown again]

Penny's examiner: Tongue choke is not a possible cause of death

Judge: We'll break.

The two medical experts are directly at odds. During the break, when Inner City

Press went out into the press pen in the hallway to take photos / video, NYC Medical Examiner walked back in with the prosecutors. Doctor Chandru said she injected speculation into her findings. What will the jury find?

XI. Penny's Medical Examiner Chandru, Homicide on Cross, Studies, Tasers & Texas

Judge: One of the jurors has a bad cold, we're going to need to take breaks. Also, I will not be releasing the transcripts of the videos to the public, since they are not in evidence. If in deliberations the jury wants them, they are going to have to come out

Jury entering!
Cross of defense medical expert Dr. Chandru.
ADA 1: I want to ask you about the alternative causes of death you propose.

There's no way to know how much K2 was in his system, right?
Dr. Chandru: It wasn't measured

ADA: K2 is like getting fearful, right?
Penny's medical expert Chandru: It can cause hallucinations
ADA: I'm asking about K2 as a possible cause of death. We're going to get back to this. Now, his schizophrenia, you say it revs him up?
Chandru: Yes

ADA: You're saying he died of sickle cell, right?
Penny's medical expert Chandru: You first have to go back and ask, did he die from a chokehold -
ADA: Let's not go back to the chokehold. What happens during the restraint?
Chandru: Your heart rate goes up

ADA: In the autopsy, his urine was clear, right?
Penny's medical expert Chandru: Yes.
ADA: There's nothing in the autopsy to

suggest he had elevated potassium, right?
Chandru: I could be.
ADA: Let's pull up the autopsy report...

[Penny's lawyer Kenniff moves back into the front row of the gallery to whisper with another there- getting ready for re-direct?]
ADA: If let's say your mentor was right & the mechanism was cardiac and not asphyxia, it wouldn't work in this case?
Chandru: It could

ADA: No one came to this courtroom and said he was breathing, right?
Penny's lawyer: Objection!
Judge Maxwell Wiley: Overruled.
Penny's lawyer: Misstates the evidence.
ADA: You gave a declaration before trial and said it was due to K2 and schizophrenia

Penny's medical expert Chandru: That was before I got the glass slides.
ADA: When did you get them?
Chandru: In October. I saw the sickling all over.
ADA: Now you've changed your mind - it's

anything but compression?

Chandru: That's not my updated declaration

ADA: There is no literature connecting K2 to the sickle of cells, correct?

[A member of the public here in the gallery seems to laugh, or whoop - a court officer goes over to shush her]

Penny's medical expert Chandru: No, there is literature, on anti-psychotics

ADA: Dr. Chandru, you've only published two articles, right?

Penny's medical expert Chandru: Yes, before being a resident.

ADA: Unlike Doctor Harris, who has published more -

Penny's lawyer: Objection.

ADA: You think you know better

ADA: You're saying you know better than the Chief Medical Examiner, than the NE Journal of Medicine-

Penny's lawyer: Objection.

Judge Wiley: Sustained. Don't answer that question.

ADA: They studied people who were stungunner or Tazed

Objection!

Overruled.

ADA: Isn't it a fact that sickle cell was being used as a way to cover up the death of African Americans in custody?

Penny's lawyer: Objection!

Judge: We're not going there.

ADA: It's relevant to the next line of questions. But let's go to the new article

ADA: This paper was intended to argue against the view that sickle cell was being used to cover up deaths of African Americans in custody?

Penny's medical expert Chandru: I don't know their intent.

ADA: These authors are mostly from Texas

ADA: 2 of these authors are advisors to a company that makes Tasers, correct?

Penny's medical expert Chandru: If you say so.

ADA: Some of the deaths in custody

attributed to sickle cell involve Tasers - that's two of them. Another author is a retired police chief

Penny's medical expert Chandru: The restraint played a role - that is different from saying he died from a chokehold. The restraint triggered a sickling event. You can call it a homicide. But it's up to the jury to decide if the restraint was appropriate

Penny's lawyer: Judge, can we have a sidebar, there's something you should know
Judge: No. Proceed.
ADA: You're saying now -
Penny's medical expert Chandru: I'm not saying anything different.

Judge: We'll break.

The cross examination brought in police brutality — noting the new study's authors' links to a Taser company - and even telling the jury of the authors being

from Texas. But Chandru's use of the term homicide, even if followed by some jury instruction, could have an impact. In the gallery, Medical Examiner Harris sat with the prosecutors

Sunny Side Up

When I put on my baseball cap
That day in May it wasn't to kill.
But when that guy got on at Second Ave
And said I'm going to kill someone,
I'll go to jail for life
I grabbed him by the neck
A hold I learned as a Marine
And soon he was still
Still breathing
Some thought

A Penny for your thoughts

www.ingramcontent.com/pod-product-compliance
Lightning Source LLC
Chambersburg PA
CBHW071653240526
45469CB00021B/2277